AUTOMOBILES

Design	Cooper – West
Editor	James McCarter
Researcher	Cecilia Weston-Baker
Consultant	Mark Chivers
Illustrator	Gerard Browne

Designed and produced by
Aladdin Books Ltd,
70 Old Compton Street,
London W1

*First published in
the United States in 1985 by*
Franklin Watts Inc
387 Park Avenue South
New York NY 10016

ISBN 0 531 10086 3

Library of Congress Catalog
Card Number: 85 10086

Printed in Belgium

MODERN TECHNOLOGY

AUTOMOBILES

DANIEL WARD

FRANKLIN WATTS

NEW YORK · LONDON · TORONTO · SYDNEY

The Turbocharged Nissan 3000 engine

Foreword

The car has been with us for just over 100 years. In that time it has developed into one of the most advanced pieces of technology that most people ever own.

There are many factors behind the drive to improve car technology. Economy has become increasingly important – car owners want good performance from their vehicles but also a low fuel consumption. Safety for passengers is even more important, and there is continuing research about the effect exhaust fumes have on our environment. Car manufacturers have responded by applying the latest technology in all areas of the vehicle – this book explains the most important new developments.

Contents

Today's vehicle	6
Electronic systems	8
Inside the engine	10
Engine power	12
Gears and transmission	14
Wheels, brakes and suspension	16
New materials	18
The drag factor	20
Safety first	22
New fuels	24
The electric car?	26
Towards 2000	28
Datechart	30
Glossary	31
Index	32

Today's vehicle

Features which are now standard on most of today's family cars, were little more than ideas ten years ago. In that short time, automobile technology has advanced so fast that a modern family sedan will outperform many older sports cars. Today's high performance sports sedans are even more impressive: the engine is turbocharged which provides plenty of power, without sacrificing fuel economy. A host of electronic "brains" monitor the engine, brakes and suspension and adjust them for the best possible combination of performance and roadholding. Four-wheel drive ensures that the power is transmitted to the road in all driving conditions, while the low profile tires give tremendous grip, for rapid cornering.

② The Engine
The engine is the powerhouse of the car. Today's engine technology has two main aims – improving the car's performance at speed and maintaining fuel economy.

① Electronics
Almost every modern car uses electronics. The miniaturized control boxes have more memory than a full-sized computer of a decade ago.

③ Materials
Plastics are being used for more than just the dash – plastic body panels make the car lighter, and plastic bumpers spring back into shape after a minor bump.

④ Transmission

Transmission carries the power from the engine to the wheels. In many modern sedans, power goes to the front wheels, but sometimes all four wheels are driven for better grip.

⑤ Safety

Unfortunately, road accidents occur all too often. Sometimes drivers are at fault, sometimes they are the result of road conditions. A properly designed interior allows the driver to concentrate on driving, and seat belts and collapsible steering columns reduce injuries in collisions.

⑥ Aerodynamics

A car isn't styled simply to look good: a smooth shape with flush windows reduces air resistance and so helps save fuel. A spoiler modifies the air flow over the rear of the car – this helps to cut down on drag, and the new air flow patterns it creates help to keep the rear window clean.

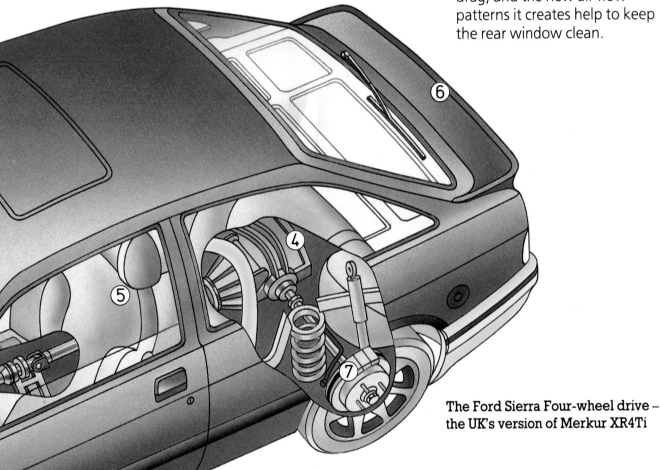

The Ford Sierra Four-wheel drive – the UK's version of Merkur XR4Ti

⑦ Brakes and Suspension

Modern cars have power-assisted disc brakes – on high performance cars, the brakes are ventilated to keep them cool. The suspension is designed to progressively stiffen as more weight is added.

The economy car

There is also a demand for a smaller economy car for everyday use. In congested cities the perfect town car would be small on the outside but quite high for good driver visibility. A highly economical three-cylinder engine powering the front wheel is ideal, and automatic transmission is suited to the stop-start conditions of city driving. Large windshields make the interior seem surprisingly roomy, and plastic bumpers protect against city knocks.

Electronic systems

Electronics are being used increasingly to make cars more efficient and reliable. Under the hood, many cars have electronic ignition to ignite the fuel/air mixture, and a few are controlled by an engine management system. In such a system, a compact central processing unit (CPU) is fed with information from sensors located in the engine. It compares the information with data stored in its memory, and adjusts the fuel and ignition systems to the best possible settings. The Ford ECU IV unit can cope with more than a million separate pieces of information every second. Electronics are also used to check on the engine's health. If a fault develops, the CPU warns the driver.

▽ On the left, the diagram shows where sensors can be located in an engine to monitor its performance, by measuring such things as temperature, fuel input and exhaust output. Below, other parts of the car where electronics are being increasingly used. Fuel level (1), the front and rear light bulbs (2), the water level in the radiator (3), and the performance of the battery and engine (4, 5) are all monitored. The information goes to collecting points (6) and is then sent to the CPU (7). This processes the data and displays it on the dashboard (8).

engine temperature

distributor

spark plug

carburettor

exhaust gases

In-car computer

Electronic driver aids are now becoming quite common. Many top-of-the-range models are fitted with a trip computer, a programmable console, into which the driver can feed information about the journey. The computer is linked to sensors which monitor the fuel flow and the car's speed. If the driver punches in the distance to go at the start of the journey, the computer will at the touch of the right button, display information on how much fuel has been used, the average speed, how far there is to go, and even the time of arrival.

▽ Today's instrument panels use electronic displays. The driver is given instant information on how the car is working. Many of the signals are relayed from sensors used to control the car's other systems.

▷ One of the most advanced electronic control systems – the Bosch Motronic. Its memory is programmed with 4096 settings for the ignition system alone. All the settings are worked out from lengthy tests in the research laboratory.

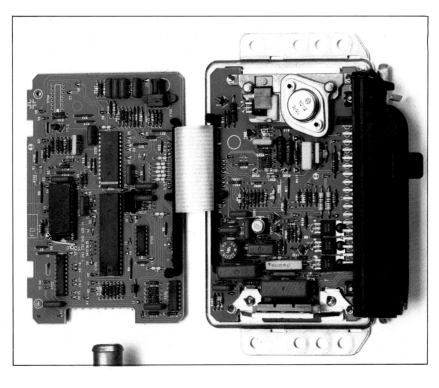

Inside the engine

The engine is the heart of the car. Inside its cylinders – most cars have four or more – a mixture of air and fuel is ignited. The force of the explosion created drives pistons which in turn drive a crankshaft. From this, power is eventually transmitted to the wheels. The efficiency of an engine depends on obtaining the correct fuel/air mixture, the exact timing of ignition and on keeping the heat lost to a minimum.

The diesel alternative

For many years, diesel has been used to fuel trucks and buses, but in Europe it is becoming an increasingly popular alternative for taxis and even family cars. The diesel engine wears less and thus has a longer engine life. Older diesel engines were slower to respond in acceleration and often noisy. The latest generation can accelerate to 62 mph (100 km/h) in just over 15 seconds, comparing favorably with equivalent gasoline-engined models.

▽ Two thoroughbred engines of a different type. On the left is the engine of a Grand Prix racing car – about ten times more powerful than that of a small family car. Right, the FIRE 1000, built by robots, with high performance capability, low fuel consumption, is designed for cheap and easy maintenance.

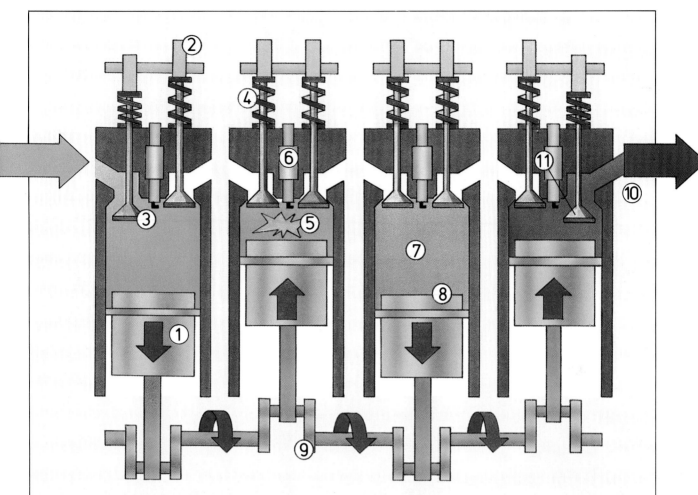

△ On the first stroke of the engine cycle, the piston (1) moves down and the camshaft (2) pushes open the inlet valve (3) to let air and fuel in. On stroke two the piston moves up to compress the fuel/air mix. A spring (4) closes the inlet valve and a spark (5) from the spark plug (6) ignites the fuel. The explosion (7) forces the piston (8) down on stroke three, turning the crankshaft (9). Stroke four forces out the exhaust gases (10) through the open exhaust valve (11).

▷ Fuel injection can greatly improve the performance and economy of an engine. Precisely regulated amounts of fuel are injected into the combustion chamber, ensuring the most efficient fuel/air mix. In some systems, the timing of the fuel injection system, and the timing of the spark from the plug, are both controlled by the same computer. This keeps both systems running at the optimum settings.

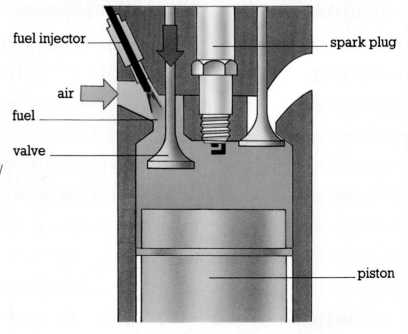

fuel injector

air

fuel

valve

spark plug

piston

Engine power

▽ The hot waste exhaust gases from the cylinders (1) pass into the exhaust side of the turbocharger, where they flow over a bladed wheel – the turbine (2) – making it spin. This spins the compressor (3). The compressor sucks in air (4) and pumps it into the intercooler (5) where it is cooled by more air flowing over the outside of the intercooler (6). As it cools, the compressed air becomes denser and takes up less space so more air gets into the cylinders. The dense air then goes to the inlet manifold (7) where it mixes with fuel before being forced into the cylinders.

To get more power from an engine, you have to improve its "breathing" – the amount of fuel/air mix that goes in, and the speed at which the exhaust comes out. The easiest way of increasing the flow, is to fit a turbocharger.

Increased power through turbocharging

A turbocharger is basically a pump, driven by the waste gases going down the exhaust pipe, which forces the fuel/air mixture into the cylinders at high pressure. The more mixture that goes in, the greater the power output of the engine – in most cases, power is increased by up to 50 per cent with a turbo. But for a turbo to work properly, other modifications are needed. Many engines have four valves per cylinder to cope with the increased gas flow.

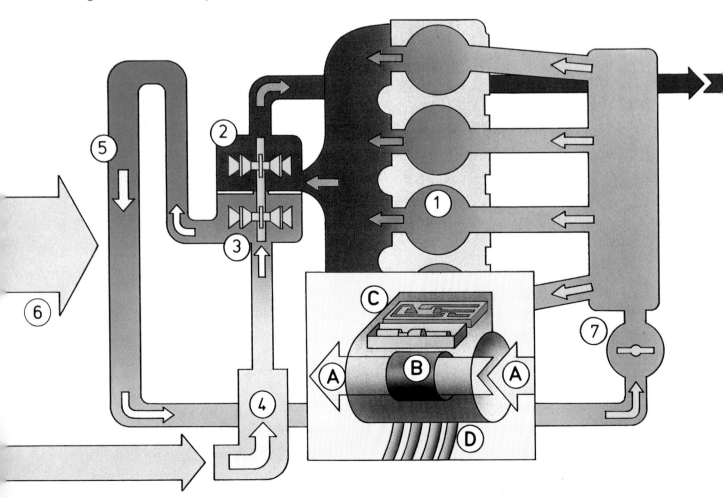

The turbocharged diesel

Diesel engines can also benefit from being turbocharged. Turbocharged trucks are commonplace, and turbo diesel cars are gaining in popularity as their performance increases. The Mercedes 300SD for example, has a top speed of 106 mph (170 km/h) and a fuel consumption of 27.5 miles per gallon (8.6 liters per 100 kms) – a good economy performance.

▽ The heat and pressures involved in a turbocharger are so great that under hard driving conditions both the exhaust and turbo will glow bright red. The bodywork near to the turbo is protected from the blistering heat by shields.

▷ The Saab 9000 Turbo engine has four valves per cylinder – this increases the amount of fuel/air mixture that the turbocharger can force into the cylinders.

◁ Inset left: an airflow meter ensures that the engine gets the right combination of fuel and air. Air going into the engine (A) passes over a heated platinum wire (B). A microprocessor (C) measures the wire's temperature. If the airflow increases, the wire cools – the microprocessor sends signals (D) to the fuel system to increase the supply.

Gears and transmission

▽ Continuously variable transmission (CVT) can keep the engine at its most efficient speed by using expanding pulleys and a drive belt. The CVT can provide any gear ratio between top gear, when the engine-driven pulley is closed up (2) and the pulley driving the wheels is fully expanded (1), and bottom gear, when the driven pulley is expanded (4) and the driving pulley is closed up (3).

Gears are needed to control the power from the engine. Typically, there are four or five forward gears and one for reverse. Lower gears are selected to give more pulling power – when a car is going uphill for example. Higher gears are used for constant cruising speeds. Traditionally the engine and gearbox were at the front of the car and turned the back wheels via a driveshaft. Weight and space can be saved by mounting the engine and gearbox across the car, driving the front wheels. With the weight of the engine over the driving wheels, grip is better on wet roads.

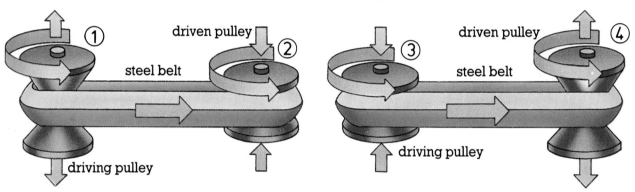

① driven pulley ② steel belt driving pulley ③ driven pulley ④ steel belt driving pulley

▽ On older cars, the engine and gearbox are at the front and in-line with the car's center. Power goes to the rear axle through the driveshaft.

Today's front-wheel drive cars have the engine and gearbox mounted across the engine bay. The rear wheels run freely and are not powered.

In four-wheel drive, the power is transmitted via two gearboxes through a series of driveshafts to both the front and rear axles.

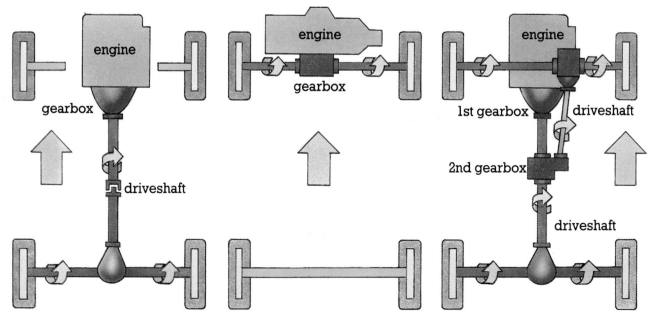

engine · gearbox · driveshaft

engine · gearbox

engine · 1st gearbox · driveshaft · 2nd gearbox · driveshaft

Ford's latest automatic gearbox – the A4LD – has four forward gears, with top being an economy gear for relaxed cruising. BMW and Mercedes also fit 4-speed auto gearboxes, and have such a high fourth gear that maximum speed is often reached in third gear.

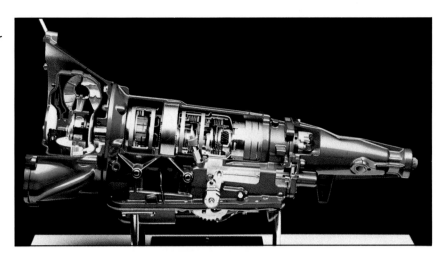

△ The Audi Quattro four-wheel drive rallying model proved outstandingly successful. It uses four-wheel drive for phenomenal levels of grip and handling, both on the road and on loose-surfaced forest tracks.

Automatic gearbox

An automatic gearbox takes much of the effort out of driving, but it does have disadvantages. Most automatic cars are slower than similar models with manual gearboxes, and tend to use more fuel too. However, the latest automatics offer good performance and economy.

Four-wheel drive

Until the last few years, four-wheel drive had only been used for off-road vehicles like Jeeps and pick-ups. It is now seen increasingly in volume production family cars.

Wheels, brakes and suspension

The vast majority of cars now have power-assisted brakes, and during an emergency stop on a wet road, it is all too easy to lock the wheels. With the wheels locked, the car goes into a skid. The latest idea is to fit an anti-lock braking system (ABS). A sensor at each wheel sends signals to an electronic control unit (ECU) indicating the speed of the wheel. The ECU senses if one wheel is slowing down too quickly, and is in danger of locking, and releases the pressure on that brake. Suspension benefits from electronic control too. The Lincoln Continental Mk VII suspension uses pressurized air instead of metal springs. Electronics constantly check the height and angle of the car. If you fill the fuel tank, the system pumps more air to the rear to keep the car level.

▷ A vivid illustration of the advantages of anti-lock braking. Without ABS, the wheels of the car on the left lock up – the car carries on in a straight line no matter which way the wheel is turned, and skids into the cones. The car on the right fitted with Mercedes ABS leaves the driver able to steer, and he avoids the cones.

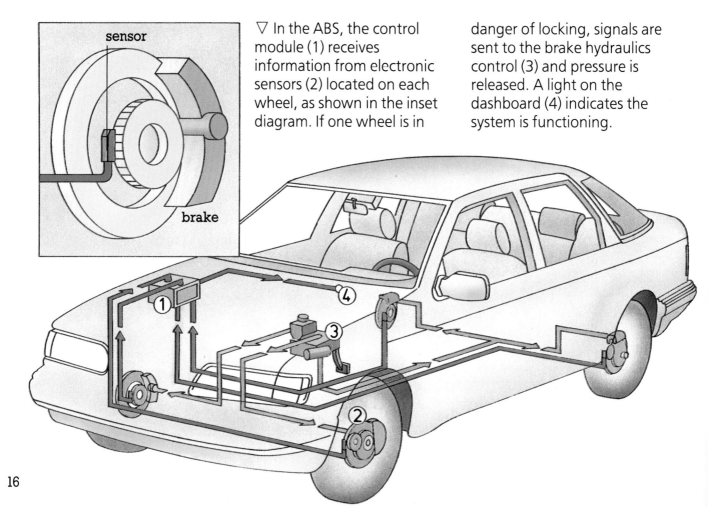

sensor

brake

▽ In the ABS, the control module (1) receives information from electronic sensors (2) located on each wheel, as shown in the inset diagram. If one wheel is in danger of locking, signals are sent to the brake hydraulics control (3) and pressure is released. A light on the dashboard (4) indicates the system is functioning.

△ The photograph on the left shows a Lotus with conventional suspension. On the right, one with active computer-controlled suspension. The active suspension stops the body rolling during hard cornering, making the car more stable.

Tire technology

The car's only contact with the road is through the tires, and as cars have become faster, tire construction has changed to keep pace. At the sort of speeds allowed on today's highways, a tire bursting can be fatal, so tire manufacturers have come up with a number of designs for "run flat" tires which allow the driver to bring the car safely to a stop after a flat. And new wider yet lower "low profile" tires have been developed which improve handling.

New materials

Steel is by far the most popular material for making cars because, above all, it is cheap. Also steel can easily be shaped and welded together for bodies and it is relatively strong for its weight. However, a switch from steel to plastic is beginning to take place when the plastic part can do the job better or costs less. For instance, there are now plastic fuel tanks because they can be molded to fit into tight corners, enabling the tank to hold more gasoline. Many new cars have large plastic bumpers which spring back undamaged after an 8 km/h (5 mph) collision – a steel bumper would stay bent.

The cost factor

The all-plastic car is still a long way off. Only by reinforcing the plastic with expensive materials like carbon fiber could it match the stiffness and strength of steel needed to make the rigid structural frame of the car.

▽ The Pontiac Fiero uses plastic body panels to achieve a considerable weight saving over previous models – every 1% of weight saved will give 0.7% better fuel economy.

▷ Modern technology has made engine research a much more exact science. A quartz window lets engineers see into the combustion chamber of an experimental engine and very precise measurements can be made by using laser light.

△ New materials: Plastic body panels and skirts (1) save weight, and an aluminum hood (2) is light and absorbs crash impacts. Seat frames (3) and other internal structures could be made of rigid plastics too, and a plastic fuel tank (4) can be molded to fit any space. In addition, axles (5) and exhaust pipes (6), could be made of glass or carbon fiber, and windows (7) of specially toughened glass.

◁ Plastic bumpers on the latest Mazda do not corrode and will spring back into shape after minor collisions.

The drag factor

Forcing a car through the air at high speed requires a lot of power; in fact at high speeds it takes about four-fifths of the engine's power. The problem is that not only is the body large but the sharp corners upset the air flow, causing turbulence and thus slowing the car. By making the body smaller and smoother, there is less drag or resistance. In this way the engine doesn't have to work so hard and uses less fuel.

Drag factors

How smooth a car's body is in the wind is measured by its drag factor. A car with a good aerodynamic body such as the latest Audi 5000-S would have a drag factor of 0.30 or less – a 1985 Cadillac Eldorado has a figure of 0.51. A shape with one of the lowest drags – 0.10 – is a teardrop, with a rounded nose, tapering to a point.

▷ A car's drag factor is measured in a wind tunnel. Huge motor-driven propellers can produce wind speeds of up to 125 mph (200 km/h). The car sits on a balance which measures the forces acting on it, and smoke trails are used to study turbulence. Inset is a computer simulation, employed in the early stages of body design.

▷ The latest UK Vauxhall Astra is a good example of the streamlined, aerodynamic design today's car manufacturers are achieving. Its features are highlighted on the opposite page.

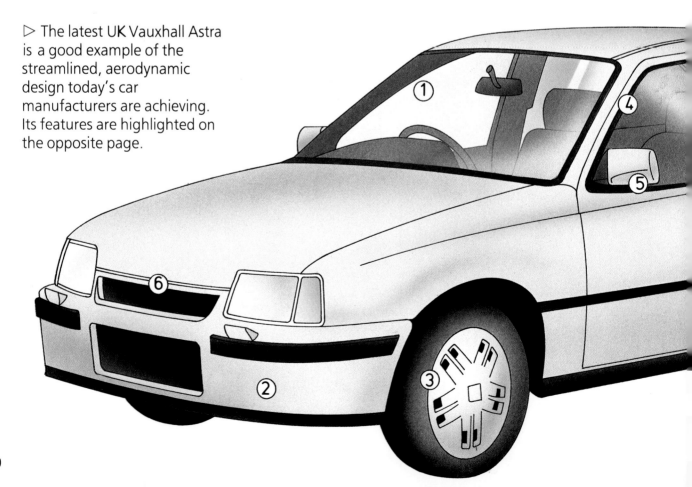

A smooth profile

Look carefully at a modern car like the Mercedes 190 and you will see that very little of the body is flat, instead the front and sides are curved. There are no sharp corners or edges and the car narrows towards the trunk. In an effort to reduce turbulence the Audi 5000-S has flush glass, where the side windows are close to the outside of the doors, making the side of the car smoother.

◁ The Astra's steeply raked windshield (1) guides air flow smoothly up and over the roof. The curved front spoiler (2) ensures a similarly smooth flow of air down the sides. Flush wheels (3) and side windows (4) and streamlined side mirrors (5) minimize turbulence here. The nose is low, – the air entering the radiator to cool the engine creates drag, so the grille (6) is kept small. The rear contour (7) is also steep, so that the air flow follows the body – if it breaks away too soon it creates turbulence and drag. Air passes above and below the rear wing (8), creating downward pressure that helps hold the car to the road and ensures that the air breaks away without causing drag.

Safety first

Improved car design can help to reduce the injuries that happen in car accidents every year. The first concern is to prevent the accident. Design features such as large windows to give the best all around view, controls positioned so that the driver's attention is not distracted from driving, do help. If the accident should happen, the interior is designed with no sharp projections, seat belts hold the occupants firmly strapped in, and the bodyshell is made to absorb the shock. The exterior is designed with the minimum of projections to cut down pedestrian injuries.

▽ A well-designed interior is an added safety factor. Controls (1) should be within easy reach of the driver, and displays (2) clearly visible. Good ventilation (3) is important for driver comfort and the seats should be adjustable (4) for all sizes of people at the wheel. Collapsible steering columns (5) are fitted to all modern cars.

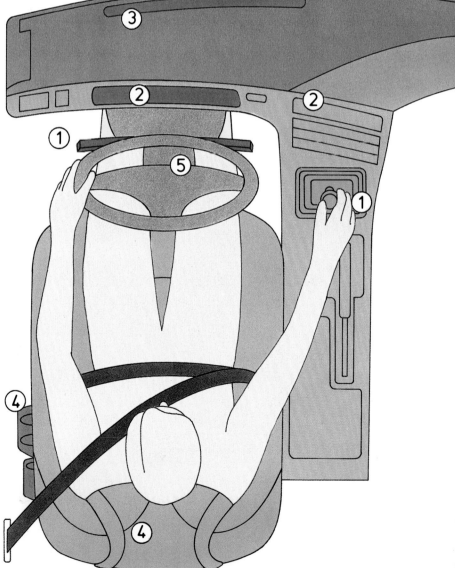

△ Air bags are a safety feature that may help save lives if they can be made to work reliably. The bag is supposed to inflate immediately in the event of a crash, activated by electronic sensors. Air bags are fitted to some cars, but have not yet proved popular.

▷ All cars undergo crash tests before they go into production. The crash is recorded on film and the car is fitted with equipment so that engineers can study exactly how it behaves under impact. In some tests special dummies, connected to a computer, are placed in the car to simulate how the passengers would behave in a crash.

△ Dash design has undergone a revolution with new electronic displays. The instruments can be clearly seen through the steering wheel and are easy to read. All this means that the driver's attention is distracted from the road for as short a time as possible. Shown here is the dash of the latest European Ford Granada.

Safety cells

Cars now have a very strong "passenger cell" in the center of the car and have the front and rear less strong. In a crash the fenders, hood and trunk will crumple and absorb energy, reducing the shock of the impact on the passengers. Collapsible steering columns and laminated windshields reduce passenger and driver injuries. Seat belts also save lives – Mercedes has developed a new seat belt that tightens automatically on impact.

New fuels

Gasoline is a very good fuel for the car because it is relatively cheap and has a high energy content. Yet there are alternative fuels. These include alcohols (ethanol and methanol) and gases.

Fuels from plants

Ethanol comes from brewing crops such as potatoes, cereals and sugar cane. Methanol is derived either from coal or is manufactured chemically. But one liter of ethanol has only two-thirds the power of one liter of gasoline.

Neither liquefied petroleum gas (LPG) nor methane are as efficient to use in car engines as gasoline. Running on these, the engine provides up to one-third less energy than on gasoline.

▽ The United States has introduced strict regulations to control pollution from car exhausts. The cars on this San Diego freeway are fitted with catalytic converters (inset) in their exhausts. These contain chemicals which remove pollutants from exhaust gases. Their disadvantage is that they reduce the power output of the engine.

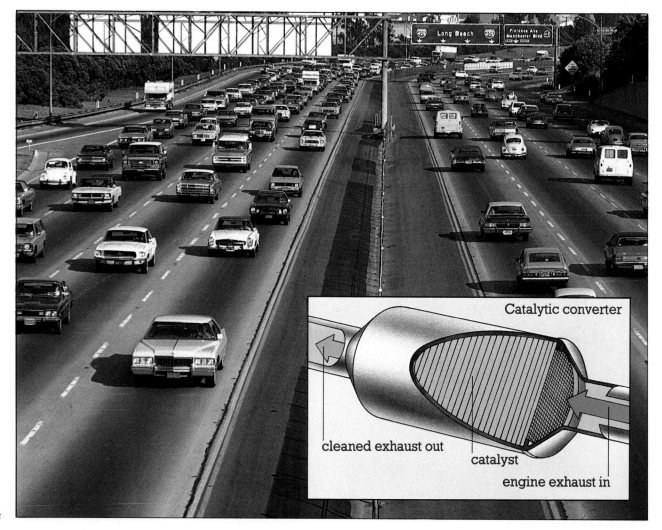

Catalytic converter

cleaned exhaust out

catalyst

engine exhaust in

The pollution factor

Carbon monoxide gas and lead are given off by car exhaust fumes, and these can present a major pollution problem. Lead is added to the gasoline to increase engine performance, but in many countries you can only get lead-free gasoline. It costs very little extra to make a car with an engine that runs on lead-free gasoline, but converting an older car to run on it can be quite expensive and performance will suffer.

▽ When oil prices rose steeply in the early 1970s, Brazil began producing alcohol fuel from plants. Today, about 40 per cent of cars in Brazil run on pure alcohol and the other 60 per cent use an alcohol/gasoline mix called gasahol.

▽ In some countries, cars are responsible for up to half of airborne pollutants – this sort of smog can be drastically reduced by using lead-free gasoline, and fitting chemical converters to the exhaust system. The cost of these changes can be high on some cars and will increase fuel consumption.

The electric car?

If supplies of fuel really do start to dwindle by about the year 2020, what sort of power will we be using for our cars? Electricity appears to be the obvious answer yet there are many problems to be solved. The only way to carry the electric power in a car is in a battery.

Drawbacks today

By comparison with gasoline today's lead/acid car battery has a poor efficiency. With just one car battery, the UK's new C5 Sinclair three-wheeler, holding only one occupant, has a limited range of about 12 miles (19 km). To recharge it takes up to eight hours compared with a matter of minutes for a gasoline-powered car. Batteries are heavy, bulky and slow to recharge. Because it is made to be kept fully charged, a battery can only withstand being drained and recharged a few hundred times. Within a short time, the battery will be exhausted and will need replacing.

▽ Two types of electric vehicle currently being developed. These cars are "hybrids" which use a combination of gasoline and electric engines. Below: in this design, power can come directly from a gasoline engine or from an electric motor powered by batteries. The most suitable power source can be selected for the type of journey.

1. Gasoline engine
2. Controller
3. Batteries
4. Electric motor
5. Driven wheel
6. Generator
7. Power source selector

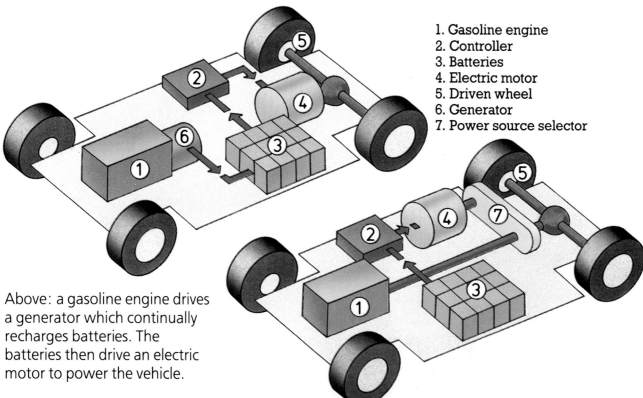

Above: a gasoline engine drives a generator which continually recharges batteries. The batteries then drive an electric motor to power the vehicle.

△ Battery-powered vehicles are ideal when high speeds and a long range are not required. The Ford Mustang above, converted to electric power, shows the large number of battery packs required, although the electric motor (inset) is relatively compact.

The electric alternative

General Motors began a project in the mid-1970s to produce a small family vehicle for town and local use. The goal was to produce a vehicle capable of a top speed of approximately 62 mph (100km/h) and with a range of 93 miles (150km).

Despite this research, the electric car is very much a thing of the future. A more likely alternative is the gasoline/electric hybrid. This would use a small gasoline engine when greater power was required. The engine would also recharge the batteries to increase the hybrid's mileage range.

Ten years on, the problem is still one of the size and weight of the battery pack needed for reasonable range and a good cruising speed.

Towards 2000

Imagine an everyday journey in the car of the future. Punch a code into the key pads on the door, it opens and then you say, "Good morning car." The car recognizes your voice and responds while automatically adjusting the seat, steering wheel and mirror to suit you. The forthcoming drive through the country lanes means the soft ride settings you selected yesterday for the drive into the city are no longer the best. You say to the car, "Sporting mode." The suspension and automatic gearbox change settings accordingly. The television screen on the dash shows the checks on the engine, lights and brakes. You are not sure of the route so you ask for a map – it is immediately displayed on the screen. Time to go, but when reverse is selected, the car will not move. The rear radar system has detected a low wall behind the car.

▷ Probe 4, Ford Motors' latest prototype model, may be the look of the car of the future. Some of its sleek styling is reflected into the Merkur XR4Ti, and the mass of electronics incorporated in it will carry on the design and technological advances seen over the last ten years.

▽ Computerized displays from Renault, one showing the driver a map of the surrounding area, the other giving an update on the state of the vehicle. Before long, such displays may be projected on the windshield, in the same way as on today's jet fighters, so that the driver can keep all attention on the road.

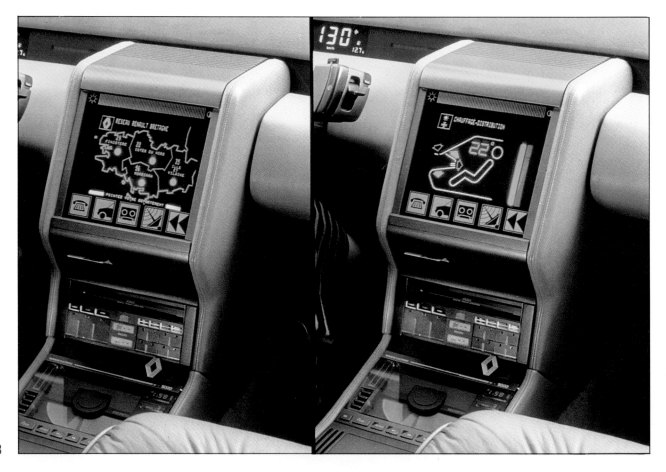

△ The Toyota company's future prototype, the FX-I. Again, economy, aerodynamic design and greater use of computer technology are the key points.

Total technology

You move forward and off on your journey. As it starts to rain, the wipers switch on automatically and the transmission selects four-wheel drive for better grip. A momentary lapse of concentration and your car is too close to the one in front. No matter, the radar assessed the danger and applied the anti-lock brakes to keep you out of trouble. The car breaks the silence by informing you that the engine has a fault. It is automatically recorded on a service card. Hand this to the garage and it will inform the service computer of the fault. All this is possible either today or in the next decade. Wait and see.

Datechart

1880

Karl Benz starts a small company producing gasoline-driven "horseless carriages," in Germany. In Britain, the first car company was Daimler, while in the US the first car company to go into production was the Duryea Motor Wagon Co., in 1896.

1898

The world land speed record is set by an electric car. Electric-powered cars hold the record for two years, reaching a top speed of about 66 mph (109 km/h) in 1899.

1908

Henry Ford begins production of the Model T. This was the first mass produced car, with a peak of over two million vehicles sold in 1923.

1911

The Indianapolis 500 race is staged for the first time. The first ever Le Mans 24-hour race was run in 1923.

September 1924

The first modern highway is opened to the public. This was a 13 miles (21 km) stretch between Milan and Varese in Italy.

1939

The German Volkswagen ("people's car") goes into production. The 20 millionth "Beetle," as the car became affectionately known, was built in Mexico in May 1981.

1958

Continuously variable transmission (CVT) is first offered on the market. It was designed by the Van Doorne brothers and used by DAF.

1959

The world's pioneering small car, the British Mini, is produced. With an economical performance, low price and good handling, the basic design changed little in its 26 years of production.

1968

The US introduces the first laws to control the emission of pollutants from car exhausts.

1974

The first "oil crisis" leads to a four-fold increase in fuel prices. This gave automobile engineers the impetus to create more economic vehicles. In the US a speed limit of 50 mph (80.5 km/h) was introduced.

January 1983

The British government introduces legislation which makes it compulsory for driver and front seat passenger to wear seat belts.

1985

Ford UK offer anti-lock braking systems as standard on their new Granada range – previously ABS was only obtainable at the more expensive end of the market.

Glossary

Active suspension	The movement of the suspension is monitored and controlled by electronics, to give the best possible combination of comfortable ride and sporting roadholding.
Catalytic converter	A special filter which is fitted into the exhaust system. It contains chemicals which remove pollutants from the exhaust gases – they are expensive and need replacing once the chemicals are exhausted.
CPU (central processing unit)	The term used for the electronic "brain" which controls a system such as the ignition, fuel or anti-lock braking. Also known as an ECU (electronic control unit).
Continuously variable transmission	A type of automatic gearbox that has no preset number of gears as in a conventional gearbox. It provides a stepless progression from bottom to top gear so that the engine can be constantly running at the most economical speed.
Low profile tires	Once the domain of high performance cars, these squat, wide tires are now seen on many less exotic cars. The "low" refers to the ratio of the tire's height, from rim to tread, to its tread width – the latest 50 series tires are half as wide as they are high.
Microprocessor	The name given to the microelectronic circuits that store and process information – in a car this takes the form of a CPU (see above).
Run flat tires	Special tires which are designed to stay on the wheel rim if they blow out so that the driver can stop the car safely. Some designs can also be driven flat for up to 50 miles at moderate speeds until a repair or replacement can be made at the driver's convenience.

Index

A

aerodynamics 7, 20, 29
Audi 15, 20-1

B

batteries 26-7
Benz, Karl 30
BMW 15
brakes 6-7, 16, 28-30

C

Cadillac Eldorado 20
catalytic converter 24, 31
CPU 8, 13, 31
computers 9, 11, 21, 23, 28-9

D

Daimler 30
drag factor 20-1
Duryea Motor Wagon Co. 30

E

ECU 8, 16, 31
electric cars 26-7, 30
electronics 6, 8-9, 16, 23, 28, 31
engine 8, 10-12, 14, 18-21, 24, 28-9, 31
    diesel 10, 13
    electric 27
    Grand Prix racing car 10
    hybrid 26-7

F

FIRE 1000 10
Ford 8, 15
    Granada 23, 30
    Model T 30
    Mustang 27
    Probe 4, 28-9
    Sierra 7
4-wheel drive 6-7, 14-15, 29
front-wheel drive 14
fuel 10-11, 24-5
    economy 5-6, 10-13, 18, 20
    injection 11

G

gears 14
General Motors 27

L

Le Mans race 30
Lotus 13, 16
Lucas 26

M

Mazda 19
Mercedes 13, 15-17, 21, 23
Merkur XR4Ti 28
Mini 30

N

Nissan 3000 4-5

P

plastics 6-7, 18-19
pollution 5, 24-5, 30-1
Pontiac Fiero 18

S

Saab 13
safety 5, 7, 22-3
seat belts 7, 22-3, 30
suspension 6-7, 16-17, 28, 31

T

tires 6, 17, 31
Toyota FX-1 29
transmission 7, 14-15, 28-9, 31
    CVT 14, 30-1
turbocharger 12-13

V

Van Doorne 30
Vauxhall Astra 20-1
Volkswagen Beetle 30

W

wheels 6-7, 10, 14, 16, 21

Acknowledgements

The publishers wish to thank the following organisations who have helped in the preparation of this book:
Autocar Magazine, British Leyland, Citroën UK, Fast Lane Magazine, Fiat Auto, Ford UK, General Motors, Johnson Mathey Chemicals. Lotus Cars, Lucas Motor Manufacturers Equipment, Mazda Cars, Mercedes Benz, Peugeot Talbot, Porsche Cars, Renault UK, Robert Bosch Ltd, Saab Great Britain, Vauxhall-Opel, Volkswagen Audi and with special thanks to Cadillac, Chevrolet, Chrysler, Buick, Ford US, Honda, Mazda, Mitsubishi, Nissan, Pontiac, Toyota.

Photographic Credits:

Cover: Porsche; *title page*: Renault; pages 4, 15, 18, 19, Autocar Magazine; page 9, A/C Delco; page 9, Robert Bosch; page 10, Fast Lane; page 10, Fiat; pages 13, 17, Lotus; page 13, Saab; pages 15, 19, 27, 29, Ford; pages 17, 21, Mercedes; pages 22, 28, Renault; page 24, Art Directors; page 25 Institute of Sugar and Alcohol; page 25, Zefa; page 29, Toyota.